CLOTHING, COSTUMES, and UNIFORMS Throughout AMERICAN HISTORY™

What People Wore
in
EARLY AMERICA

∞ Allison Stark Draper ∞

The Rosen Publishing Group's
PowerKids Press™
New York

For my mother

Published in 2001 by The Rosen Publishing Group, Inc.
29 East 21st Street, New York, NY 10010

First Edition

Book Design: Emily Muschinske

Photo Credits: p. 3 © Art Resource; p. 4, 5, 7, 17 © Archive Photos; pp. 5, 9, 14, 17, 19, 20, 21 courtesy of *Historic Dress in America* by Elizabeth McClellan/illustrations © Sophie B. Steel; p. 7, 8, 13, 15 © North Wind Picture Archives; p.10, 11, 12 © SuperStock; p. 15 © Thaddeus Harden; p. 17 © National Portrait Gallery, London/SuperStock.

Draper, Allison Stark.
    What people wore in early America / by Allison Stark Draper.
      p. cm.— (Clothing, costumes, and uniforms throughout American history)
    Summary: Describes what people wore in early America, discussing colonial, Puritan, and Native American styles.
    ISBN 0-8239-5664-4 (alk. paper)
    1. Costume—United States—History—Juvenile literature. [1. Costume—History.] I. Title. II. Series.

GT607 .D73 2000
391'.00973—dc21   00-024764

Contents

Copying a King

In 1607, a group of 144 English **settlers** arrived in America. These were the first English settlers in this new land. Their ship landed in the **colony** of Virginia. The men named the town they settled in Jamestown, after King James I of England. The settlers dressed in the style of clothes that they had worn in England. In England the best tailors sewed clothes for the royal family. King James I dressed in a jacket called a doublet. The doublet was **fitted** and had a high collar. The king also wore baggy, padded shorts called trunk hose. Under the trunk hose, he wore bright stockings that had patterns sewn into them. The rich men in England and in the American colonies dressed like the king.

In this picture of King James I, he is wearing a stiff lace collar called a ruff. Rich men and women wore this kind of collar. They wanted to dress like the king.

Working people wore flat collars instead of ruffs. The men in this picture are also wearing doublets and trunk hose.

Native American Clothing

There were thousands of Native American groups in North America. Each group had its own way of dressing. Native American clothing was very different from British clothing. The Native Americans made clothes from animal skins instead of from cloth. They scraped the fur from the skins of deer, elk, and moose. Sometimes the Native Americans decorated the skins with **dyed** porcupine feathers.

Native American women wore dresses. In the winter, they also wore **leggings** that tied at the knees. They wore shoes called **moccasins**. Native American men wore shirts, long leggings, short skirts called breechcloths, and moccasins. For important occasions, Native Americans wore **ceremonial** clothes. Different groups had different styles of ceremonial dress. These clothes were often decorated with **quills** and feathers.

These Native American moccasins are decorated with colored beads. The Native American man on the right is wearing a breechcloth.

6

Styles Change Slowly

The American colonists in Jamestown wanted to dress like people in England. England was far from America, though. It took months to hear of new styles. Clothes also cost a lot of money. All cloth was sewn by hand. Only rich people could buy new clothes every year.

People with less money changed their clothing styles slowly. The farmers and working people in Jamestown wore the same clothes for years. They even passed down clothes to their children and grandchildren. A special piece of clothing, like a fur hat or a coat with a silver **clasp**, could be passed down in a family for 100 years.

Most little girls had only one fancy dress. They wore an apron over the dress so the dress would not get dirty.

The man in this picture is wearing a doublet like the one King James I wore. His pointy beard is also like the king's. The woman's clothes copy the royal family, too. She is wearing a collar called a ruff.

8

Dressing Like Their Parents

The children of colonists wore dresses called gowns until they were seven or eight years old. In the winter, these gowns were made out of wool. When the weather turned warmer, the boys and girls wore gowns made from cotton or linen. The gowns had full-length skirts and long-sleeved shirts. At the age of eight or nine, boys stopped wearing gowns. They started to dress more like their fathers and older brothers. Girls began to wear dresses that were more like the dresses worn by their mothers.

 When they stopped wearing gowns, girls wore long dresses and caps to cover their head.

As boys got older they stopped wearing gowns. They began to dress like their brothers and fathers.

10

Plain and Simple

The first British people to settle in Massachusetts were called **Pilgrims**. The Pilgrims left England because they were not free to **worship** God the way they wanted. Their boat docked in Plymouth, Massachusetts in 1620. The first winter in Plymouth was very hard. Half of the Pilgrims died. Those that lived were very poor. They dressed in simple clothes that did not cost a lot of money to make.

Many pictures of Pilgrims show them wearing black and white clothes. Pilgrims wore black and white to church and for special occasions. Most of the time they wore many different colors. Some of the colors the Pilgrims wore were red, green, brown, blue, violet, and gray.

Pilgrims did not always wear black and white clothes. They wore these colors to church and for special occasions. Most of the time they dressed in brighter colors, though.

Pilgrims Dress With Respect for God

Pilgrim women wore undershirts made of linen. They wore **petticoats** under their skirts that reached their ankles. Pilgrim women wore cotton in the summer and wool in the winter. Sometimes the sleeves of their shirts were separate pieces that attached with ribbons. Sometimes the sleeves were sewn to the shirts. Pilgrim women wore hats at all times. They felt that covering their heads was a sign of respect for God. Pilgrim men wore linen shirts with collars. They wore close-fitting jackets that buttoned down the front. They wore loose pants called breeches that came down to the knee. In the winter, men wore felt coats and hats. Felt is a cloth made out of fur and wool.

The sleeves on women's dresses were often separate pieces that were attached with ribbons.

Pilgrim women covered their heads with a cap. They believed this was a sign of respect for God.

This picture shows a Pilgrim woman spinning wool into yarn to make clothes for the winter.

Cavalier Clothing

In the 1640s, there was a **civil war** in England. People called **Cavaliers** supported King Charles I, who was the king at that time. In the American colonies, 3,000 miles from England, there were also Cavaliers.

Cavalier men wore very fancy clothes. They wore collars made of lace. Their shirts were made of brightly colored cloth. Men cut slits in the sleeves of their jackets to show off the shirts they had on underneath. They wore hats that had long feathers on them. Many men shaved their heads and wore long, curly wigs. Sometimes they wore linen caps instead of wigs. They kept the wigs on head-shaped stands. The wigs had to be sent out to have **lice** eggs removed from them. These eggs were tiny. They were called nits.

Cavalier men wore long, curly wigs like the one shown in this picture.

The Cavalier man in this picture is wearing boots called bucket boots. Bucket boots got their name because the boot's wide top looks like a bucket.

This is a picture of King Charles I of England. There are slits cut into his jacket to show off the brightly colored shirt underneath.

Cavalier Women

Cavalier women dressed in even fancier clothes than Cavalier men. They wore **brocade** gowns. The upper parts of these gowns were called bodices. The bodices tied tightly in the back. Cavalier women also wore full skirts and long, puffy sleeves. They wore huge lace collars. Dresses were decorated with lace and feathers. Women carried beautiful silk fans.

Cavalier women also liked having fancy hairdos. They piled their hair high on their heads. They curled tight **ringlets** around their faces. They pinned **ornaments** shaped like flowers, birds, and fruit to their hair. The women were careful to protect themselves from the weather. Special umbrellas called parasols protected them from the sun. They wore lace scarves around their hair when it was windy.

Cavalier women wore their hair in tight ringlets. They wore full sleeves on their dresses and decorated them with fabric such as lace.

This Cavalier woman is wearing a dress made from red silk. The sleeves of the dress are slashed to show the shirt underneath. The collar she has on is made of lace.

The Puritans

The **Puritans** and Cavaliers disagreed about who should rule England. The Cavaliers supported King Charles I. The Puritans were supporters of Oliver Cromwell. Cromwell did not trust the Church of England, which was run by King Charles I. In the American colony of Virginia, there were more Cavaliers than there were Puritans. The Puritans did not want to be attacked because of their beliefs. Sometimes they tried to dress like the Cavaliers so that they would not be recognized.

Puritans did not believe in wearing fancy clothes. They dressed in plain fabrics and did not use lace or any other decorations on their clothes.

In the colony of Massachusetts, there were more Puritans than there were Cavaliers. The Puritans in Massachusetts felt free to dress the way they wanted. Their clothes were plainer than Cavalier clothes. They did not use lace and fancy fabric. Some Puritan men wore their hair in a round fringe. Their hair looked like someone had put a soup bowl on their head and cut around it. In England Puritans who wore their hair this way were called Round Heads.

The Cavaliers dressed in fancier clothes than the Puritans. They came to America to make money and they liked to show off their wealth. The Puritans came to America for religious freedom. They thought that wearing fancy clothes did not show respect for God.

Early American Soldiers

Early American soldiers had their own way of dressing. Sometimes they wore **armor**. It was no longer in style to wear whole suits of armor. Armor was heavy. This made it hard for soldiers to move and fight. Instead early American soldiers wore separate metal plates on their backs and chests. They also wore armor to protect their thighs. They wore helmets to protect their heads. By 1650, soldiers did not wear armor at all. They wore thick coats that could stop a sword from cutting their body. They also wore tough leather breeches to protect their legs.

As the British settled in America, they brought over different styles from England. They also changed some of their clothing styles to **adapt** to their new land and lifestyles. Settlers would continue to do this throughout American history.

Glossary

adapt (uh-DAPT) To change to fit new conditions.

armor (AR-mer) A type of uniform used in battle to help protect the body.

brocade (bro-KAYD) A fancy fabric with designs sewn on it in thread.

Cavaliers (ka-vuh-LEERS) British people in England or the colonies who supported King Charles I.

ceremonial (sehr-ih-MOH-nee-ul) Having to do with a ceremony.

civil war (SIH-vul WOR) A war between two sides within one country.

clasp (KLASP) Something used to hold two objects together.

colony (KAH-luh-nee) An area in a new country where a large group of people move who are still ruled by the leaders of the old country.

dyed (DYD) Colored.

fitted (FIH-tid) Shaped for an exact fit.

leggings (LEH-geengz) Coverings for the leg.

moccasins (MAH-kuh-sinz) Indian shoes made of leather and often decorated with beads.

lice (LYS) Small insects that live on people's heads.

ornaments (OR-nuh-ments) Decorations such as pins or jewelry.

petticoats (PEH-tee-kohts) Underskirts that are usually a little shorter than a woman's outer clothing.

Pilgrims (PIL-grimz) People who came to America from England in 1620 on the *Mayflower*.

Puritans (PYUR-ih-tenz) People in the 1500s and 1600s who belonged to the Protestant religion.

quills (KWILLZ) Large stiff feathers.

ringlets (RING-lets) Long curls of hair.

settlers (SEH-tuh-lerz) People who move to a new land to live.

worship (WUR-ship) To pay great honor and respect to someone or something.

Index

Web Sites

To find out more about Early American Clothing, check out these Web sites:
http://www.thehistorynet.com
http://www.jefferson.village.virginia.edu/vodh/jamestown/contents.html